Friendship
Therapy

Friendship Therapy

written by
**Kass P. Dotterweich
and John D. Perry**

illustrated by
R.W. Alley

 **ABBEY PRESS**

Text © 1994 Kass P. Dotterweich and John D. Perry
Illustrations © 1994 St. Meinrad Archabbey
Published by One Caring Place
Abbey Press
St. Meinrad, Indiana 47577

Library of Congress Catalog Number
93-074868

ISBN 978-0-87029-270-5

Printed in the United States of America

Foreword

Friendship is the cornerstone of life, the "place" where we can be ourselves, even as we're becoming our best. Yet, when demanding schedules and daily responsibilities distract us from appreciating life's most priceless gifts, we sometimes neglect to cultivate friendship.

Take a moment to think about a favorite friend. Why is this person your friend? Have you told your friend that the relationship you share is important to you—and why? Are there ways you can enrich that relationship?

Friendship Therapy can help you appraise your friendship with honesty and objectivity, appreciate and validate the unique relationship you have with your friend, and enhance your ability to be a friend. As a gift for someone else, it can provide a way to express caring sentiments that are sometimes difficult to articulate and can serve as a testimonial to the value of your relationship.

Let the insights of *Friendship Therapy* be your "friendly" guide to the riches of sharing your deepest self in the gift of friendship.

1.

A friend accepts you just as you are. Who you are in your friend's eyes gives you a glimpse of who you are in God's eyes.

2.

Cultivate your friendship. In the soil of respect, drenched with the light of truth and the moisture of compassion, life will burst forth as a towering tree, abundant with the fruit of love.

3.

Let your friendship be large or small, tall or short, square or round, paisley or plain. Friendships come in every size and shape and shade imaginable.

4.

Allow your friendship the graceful freedom of a ship at sea. When the waves dash against you, when the strong winds fill your sails, when the calm allows clear sailing, when the stars guide you by night, you are partners at the helm. Your friend-ship can take you to distant and undreamed-of shores.

5.

To be a good friend, value yourself. To treasure another's essence in your heart, you must first treasure the precious essence that is you.

6.

You don't need to vow to be a friend forever; just be. Say yes to the gift you are to each other and warm yourselves in the glow of that miracle.

7.

Give to your friend without expecting something in return. The most gratifying giving comes without expectation or concern for outcome.

8.

Spend time with your friend:
sweet time—walking, playing,
praying; not-so-sweet time—
disagreeing, hurting, searching.
Friendship embraces the whole
spectrum of life itself.

9.

Listen gleefully to each other's laughter; your hearts will know abundant joy.

10.

Listen gently to each other's
sobs; your hearts will know
abundant life.

11.

Bless your friend's brokenness;
let your friend bless yours. This
is what God does.

12.

Accept your friend without being judgmental. It's not that you don't challenge each other; it's just that you strive to know each other's reality.

13.

Turn to your friend when you're feeling weak or in need of help. You may have more to offer the relationship when it seems you have little to give.

14.

Let your friend be weak or in need; a friend's weakness is a gift that calls out to your strength.

15.

Be truthful with your friend.
Truth and love are themselves
friends; one without the other
makes each less.

16.

Be humble with your friend.
You cannot be who your friend
needs if you think you have all
the answers.

17.

Allow yourself to be loved by your friend. You can give only what you have received. When your friend knocks on the door of your heart with love, put out the welcome mat of your longing-to-be-loved self.

18.

Be open to finding new aspects of your true self in your friendship. When you see yourself in the eyes of a friend, you discover "you" as a fresh and exciting creation.

19.

Do not compete with your friend; play, but do not compete. Friendship does not have a goal—and "winning" or "beating" is a goal.

20.

Don't falsely flatter your friend because you're trying to avoid being critical. There's another way—being affirming while expressing constructive, loving concern.

21.

Don't fear the anger that is a natural part of friendship. Anger itself can be a friend telling you that something is wrong. Respond with openness and honesty.

22.

When your friend hurts you,
your friendship can survive.
Don't try to hide your pain.
Talk it over. And enjoy the
delightful effervescence of
reconciliation.

23.

Share a special time with your friend—an early morning breakfast, a walk at sunset, a late-night conversation. When your souls are free from the day's concerns, you can savor the quiet bond between you.

24.

Touch your friend. When it is respectful and reassuring, not needy and demanding, touch between friends is sacred, connecting body and soul.

25.

Accept a friend's departure
gracefully. Farewells allow for
new beginnings and fresh
experiences. You will have that
much more to give one another
when you come together again.

26.

Appreciate the time you spend away from your friend. If time apart seems to threaten your friendship, examine what your real concerns are and how you can deal with them.

27.

When overtures of friendship
are made in ways that make
you uncomfortable, your friend
is probably needy. Give your
friend a chance to explore that
neediness by being honest about
your discomfort.

28.

Say "no" to your friend when "no" is appropriate, and gracefully accept your friend's "no." Friendship is wide enough and deep enough to allow "no," "yes," "maybe," and "I don't know."

29.

Respect your own boundaries
as well as your friend's. Not
everything inside you needs
exposing. Know what is yours
to share and what is yours to
hold quietly within.

30.

When you stand on the shoulders of a friend, more is visible. When you stand back to back, there is less to fear. When you stand shoulder to shoulder, the load is lighter. And when you gaze upward together, the grandeur of the sky is breathtaking.

31.

Welcome magic and serendipity in your friendship. The most wonderful things can happen when two persons share their deepest selves.

32.

Let the radiance of your friendship pour through each of you like light through a prism. Together you create a rainbow that the world would not otherwise know.

33.

Pray with your friend and speak of God together. The most profound experience in friendship is to share your encounters with Mystery.

34.

Set an anniversary date to mark the birth of your friendship. Together you can remember, laugh, cry, and dream about the future.

35.

Celebrate your friendship with gratitude. Lift up your friend in thanksgiving and rejoice in God's blessing.

Kass P. Dotterweich and **John D. Perry**'s friendship embraces their marriage, blended family, and work. Kass is managing editor of Triumph Books, an imprint of Liguori Publications. John is a social worker for the St. Louis County Family Court.

Illustrator for the Abbey Press Elf-help Books, **R.W. Alley** also illustrates and writes children's books. He lives in Barrington, Rhode Island, with his wife, daughter, and son. See a wide variety of his works at: www.rwalley.com.

The Story of the Abbey Press Elves

The engaging figures that populate the Abbey Press "elf-help" line of publications and products first appeared in 1987 on the pages of a small self-help book called *Be-good-to-yourself Therapy*. Shaped by the publishing staff's vision and defined in R.W. Alley's inventive illustrations, they lived out author Cherry Hartman's gentle, self-nurturing advice with charm, poignancy, and humor.

Reader response was so enthusiastic that more Elf-help Books were soon under way, a still-growing series that has inspired a line of related gift products.

The especially endearing character featured in the early books—sporting a cap with a mood-changing candle in its peak—has since been joined by a spirited female elf with flowers in her hair.

These two exuberant, sensitive, resourceful, kindhearted, lovable sprites, along with their lively elfin community, reveal what's truly important as they offer messages of joy and wonder, playfulness and co-creation, wholeness and serenity, the miracle of life and the mystery of God's love.

With wisdom and whimsy, these little creatures with long noses demonstrate the elf-help way to a rich and fulfilling life.

Elf-help Books

...adding "a little character" and a lot of help to self-help reading!

Book price is $4.95 unless otherwise noted.
Available at your favorite gift shop or bookstore—
or directly from One Caring Place, Abbey Press
Publications, St. Meinrad, IN 47577.
Or call 1-800-325-2511.
www.carenotes.com